IF YOU'RE CITY
IF YOU'RE COUNTRY

EARL DIBBLES JR.

BMG

IF YOU'RE CITY, IF YOU'RE COUNTRY

Illustrations by Patrick Biederer
Design by Shauna & Sarah Dodds, Backstage Design Studio
Additional content contributions by Frank Rogers, Tyler Smith, and Chris Lee
Book production services by Adept Content Solutions

Library of Congress Cataloging-in-Publication Data available upon request.

ISBN: 9781947026162

Published by BMG
www.bmg.com

IF YOU'RE **COUNTRY**...

FAST FOOD IS NOT PERFECT
IF YOU'RE IN A BIG HURRY TO EAT.
(AVOID DEER AND STICK WITH SLOWER FOOD, LIKE TURTLES.)

IF YOU'RE **COUNTRY**...

YOU PROBABLY LOVE *JAMS*.

IF YOU'RE CITY...

YOU CAN BROWSE THE WEB
FOR ALL SORTS OF THINGS:
SHOPPING, GAMES, SPORTS, DATING...

IF YOU'RE CITY...

A BRIEFCASE IS A MAN PURSE USED FOR CARRYING LAPTOPS, LIP BALM AND TANNING CREAM.

IF YOU'RE COUNTRY...

SOMETIMES POISON IVY ITCHES FOR A WEEK, AND SOMETIMES IT GOES AWAY IN ONE DAY. IF YOU GET A **BRIEF CASE** OF ITCHIN', YOU'RE LUCKY!

IF YOU'RE **COUNTRY**...

A 10 LB BASS...NOW THAT'S **GRATE!**

IF YOU'RE COUNTRY...

AND HER DADDY DOESN'T LIKE YOU TOO MUCH, FIND A SPOT DOWN THE ROAD FROM HER HOUSE. JUST *PARK AN' MEET HER*

IF YOU'RE CITY...

A GOOD NETWORK IS GREAT WHEN YOU NEED TO DOWNLOAD A BIG FILE.

IF YOU'RE COUNTRY...

GOOD *NET WORK* IS GREAT WHEN
YOU NEED TO UPLOAD A BIG BASS
INTO THE BOAT.

IF YOU'RE CITY...

THE TRAFFIC IS USUALLY TOO BAD TO DRIVE, AND YOU NEED ANOTHER WAY TO GET TO YOUR CITY JOB. BETTER **TRAIN IT** TO WORK.

IF YOU'RE COUNTRY...

AND THAT PUPPY DON'T KNOW HOW
TO FETCH A BEER YET,
BETTER **TRAIN IT** TO WORK.

SKINNY JEAN'S THE GIRL ONE
TOWN OVER WHO'S SO GOOD WITH
A STICK SHIFT. MAN, SHE IS PRETTY!

MOHAWKS ARE A HAIRSTYLE
FOR THOSE CITY FOLK
WHO FEEL LIKE THEY'RE A LITTLE BIT
MORE ROOSTER THAN CHICKEN.

CORN ROWS ARE A HAIRSTYLE
THAT SEPARATES THE HAIR IN ROWS
SO CITY FOLK CAN EASILY
CHECK FOR LICE.

A **HIPSTER** IS THE KIND OF CITY BOY YOU FIND IN THE DARK CORNER OF THE COFFEE SHOP. THEY LIKE ORGANIC BEARD OIL AND VINYL RECORDS.

IF YOU'RE COUNTRY...

GRANDPA PROBABLY WARNED YOU ABOUT DOIN' THE **HIP STIR** TOO YOUNG. IT'S BEST TO WAIT UNTIL MARRIAGE.

A **SMART CAR** IS A VEHICLE THAT LOOKS AND SOUNDS LIKE A TOY.

IF YOU'RE COUNTRY...

A SMART CAR IS ANY CAR THAT PULLS ONTO THE SHOULDER TO LET A PICKUP TRUCK PASS.

IF YOU'RE CITY...

AND YOU WANT TO KEEP TRACK
OF ALL THE UNSWEET TEA YOU DRINK,
YOU CAN PUT IT ON A THING CALLED
A SPREADSHEET.

IF YOU'RE COUNTRY...

YOU KNOW A SPREAD IS THE LENGTH OF A BUCK'S ANTLER WIDTH. IF YOU WANT TO WRITE THAT NUMBER DOWN TO BRAG TO YOUR BUDDIES, YOU CAN PUT IT ON A THING CALLED A **SPREADSHEET**.

IF YOU'RE COUNTRY...

WHEN YOUR SWEETIE FINDS AN OLD LOVE
LETTER FROM YOUR EX-GIRLFRIEND,
JUST TELL HER THAT WAS **PRE-US**.

IF YOU'RE COUNTRY...

WHEN YOU DON'T KNOW YOUR NEIGHBOR TOO GOOD, AND THERE'S NO FISH IN HIS POND, BRING OVER A BAG OF BABY CATFISH. TOGETHER, YOU CAN **STOCK** & **BOND**.

A **PROFIT** IS THE MONEY YOU WON'T MAKE SELLING YOUR USED PENNY LOAFERS TO THE THRIFT STORE.

IF YOU'RE COUNTRY...

A **PROFIT** IS THE FORTUNE TELLER
AT THE COUNTY FAIR.

IF YOU'RE **CITY**...

A **NET PROFIT** IS THE MONEY YOU WON'T MAKE SELLING YOUR USED SMART CAR MINUS THE $300 YOU PAID FOR IT BRAND NEW.

IF YOU'RE COUNTRY...

A **NET PROFIT** IS THE FORTUNE
TELLER AT THE COUNTY FAIR WHO
SPECIALIZES IN FISHIN'.

A **GROSS PROFIT** IS THE MONEY YOU WON'T MAKE SELLING YOUR USED SKINNY JEANS TO THE THRIFT STORE INCLUDING THE $400 YOU PAID FOR THEM BRAND NEW.

IF YOU'RE COUNTRY...

A GROSS PROFIT IS THE NASTY, SMELLY FORTUNE TELLER AT THE COUNTY FAIR.

SOME JOBS MAKE YOU SELL A CERTAIN AMOUNT OF CITY THINGS EACH YEAR. I'M PRETTY SURE THAT'S A QUOTA.

IF YOU'RE COUNTRY...

TWO DIMES PLUS A NICKEL. I'M PRETTY
SURE THAT EQUALS A **QUOTA**.

IF YOU'RE **CITY**...

AND YOU WANT A HEAPING SERVING
OF INTERNET, *LOG ON.*
WHEN YOU'RE DONE, *LOG OFF.*

IF YOU'RE COUNTRY...

AND YOU WANT TO SIT DOWN, *LOG ON.*
WHEN YOU'RE DONE, *LOG OFF.*

IF YOU'RE CITY...

SOFTWARE MAKES YOUR LIFE MUCH EASIER.

IF YOU'RE COUNTRY...

SOFTWARE *MAKES YOUR LIFE MUCH EASIER. NO ONE LIKES ROUGH UNDIES THAT CHAFE. THE SOFTER THE BETTER!*

IF YOU'RE CITY...

AND YOU SPEND A LOT OF TIME WEB SURFING ON YOUR SMART PHONE, YOU BETTER HAVE A GOOD DATA PLAN.

IF YOU'RE COUNTRY...

AND YOU SPEND A LOT OF TIME HIP STIRRIN' IN THE HAYLOFT, YOU BETTER HAVE A GOOD *DADA PLAN!*

IF YOU'RE **CITY**...

THE FIRST THING YOU NEED TO GET YOUR COMPUTER ONLINE IS A **MODEM**.

IF YOU'RE COUNTRY...

THEN PASS ME THOSE BARBECUE CHICKEN WINGS! I WANT SUM *MO' DEM!*

IF YOU'RE CITY...

RUNWAYS ARE LONG STRIPS OF CONCRETE WHERE AIRPLANES LAND.

IF YOU'RE COUNTRY...

THERE ARE ALL KINDS OF DIFFERENT **RUNWAYS**. IT JUST DEPENDS ON WHICH WAY YOU NEED TO RUN. USE A FAST RUNWAY WHEN YOU SEE A RATTLESNAKE!

SHOOTING THE BREEZE IS
WHAT YOU DO DURING YOUR
LUNCH BREAK AT THE JUICE BAR.

4x4 EQUALS 16.

IF YOU'RE **COUNTRY**...

4x4 EQUALS THE ONLY WAY OUT OF THE MUD HOLE.

IF YOU'RE COUNTRY...

OOH BURR IS SOMETHING YOU SAY IN THE DEER STAND IN DECEMBER.

AND YOU ARE WONDERING WHO'S THAT POP SINGER WITH THE BIG HAIR AND SAGGY UNDERPANTS? OH, THAT'S **JUST A BEAVER.**

IF YOU'RE COUNTRY...

AND YOU'RE WONDERIN' WHAT WAS THAT
SPLASH OVER THERE IN THE CREEK?
OH, THAT'S **JUST A BEAVER.**

IF YOU'RE CITY...

SOMETIMES IT'S BEST TO STEER CLEAR
OF **POLITICS**. GET TOO CLOSE, AND IT CAN
BITE YOU IN THE BUTT.

IF YOU'RE COUNTRY...

SOMETIMES IT'S BEST TO STEER CLEAR OF **POLITICS**. A TICK IS BAD ENOUGH BY ITSELF, BUT A PILE OF 'EM IS WAY WORSE!

IF YOU'RE **CITY**...

AND YOU LIKE HOUSES LINED UP NEATLY IN A ROW AND YOUR NEIGHBORS CLOSE, YOU SHOULD LIVE IN A **NEIGHBORHOOD**.

IF YOU'RE **CITY**...

AN **APARTMENT** IS ONE OF THE ONLY
PLACES YOU CAN LIVE. THERE'S NO
HOUSES IN THE CITY.

SOMETIMES CHEWIN' TOBACCO IS BETTER MIXED TOGETHER: A PART WINTERGREEN AND **A PART MINT.**

IF YOU'RE CITY...

AND YOU WANT SOMETHING KINDA LIKE AN APARTMENT, KINDA LIKE A LOFT, BUT YOU WANT TO OWN ALL 100 SQUARE FEET OF IT, YOU WANT A *CONDOMINIUM*.

IF YOU'RE **CITY**...

A **LOFT** IS A PLACE TO LIVE
THAT'S KINDA LIKE A HALF APARTMENT
WITH A COOLER NAME.

IF YOU'RE CITY...

AND YOU'RE MAD THAT YOU DON'T HAVE ENOUGH MONEY LEFT OVER FOR BANANA SMOOTHIES, SAY THANK YOU TO YOUR *LANDLORD*.

IF YOU'RE **CITY**...

A *COLD SHOULDER* IS WHAT YOU GET FROM A HIPSTER WHEN YOU FORGET HIS GREEN TEA.

IF YOU'RE CITY...

SOMETIMES YOU CAN'T PAY FOR YOUR SMART CAR ALL AT ONCE, SO YOU'LL NEED A **BANK NOTE**.

SOMETIMES YOU FIND THE PERFECT FISHIN'
HOLE AND DON'T WANT NO ONE TO TAKE
YOUR SPOT WHEN YOU GO TO LUNCH.
YOU'LL NEED A **BANK NOTE**. JUST WRITE
IT AND LEAVE IT ON THE RIVER BANK.

IF YOU'RE CITY...

YOU USUALLY HAVE FULL BARS. CELL SERVICE IS PRETTY GOOD IN THE CITY.

IF YOU'RE CITY...

AND YOU NEED A RETIREMENT PLAN, GET A 401K.

IF YOU'RE COUNTRY...

AND YOU NEED DIRECTIONS TO THE
FIELD PARTY, GO 'BOUT A MILE PAST THE
CREEK, CROSS THE CATTLE GUARD, THEN
TURN LEFT ON COUNTY ROAD 401, K?

IF YOU'RE **CITY**...

A SKYLINE IS THE VIEW OF TALL BUILDINGS IN THE DISTANCE. IT SYMBOLIZES ABOUT AS CLOSE AS A COUNTRY BOY WANTS TO GET TO THE CITY.

A **SKYLINE** IS THAT LINE IN THE SKY THAT LOOKS LIKE A SKINNY CLOUD. IT'S NOT A GOVERNMENT COVER-UP; IT'S ACTUALLY FROM AIRPLANES! (AND ALIENS)

THERE ARE CERTAIN COFFEE SHOPS
THAT SELL SMALL CUPS OF COFFEE,
BUT SAY THEY'RE TALL.

IF YOU'RE COUNTRY...

YOU'VE PROBABLY KILLED A LOT OF
GOOD BUCKS IN YOUR LIFE. BUT YOU KNOW
THOSE COUPLE OF DEER SO GREAT THAT
YOU HUNG 'EM ABOVE YOUR WATERBED?
THOSE ARE YOUR **STAR BUCKS**.

A MAN AT THE BANK WHO CAN SELL YOU
EXPENSIVE PIECES OF PAPER IS A **BROKER**.

IF YOU'RE **COUNTRY**...

AND YOU'RE POORER THAN YOU WERE YESTERDAY, YOU'RE **BROKER**.

IF YOU'RE CITY...

YOU CAN FIND A HOT SPOT AND CONNECT YOUR PHONE.

IF YOU'RE COUNTRY...

YOU CAN FIND A **HOT SPOT** AND CONNECT
A BAND-AID. THEN CHANGE SOCKS
BEFORE IT TURNS INTO A PESKY BLISTER.

IF YOU'RE CITY...

EVERYBODY LOVES CHASING A *BUCK*.

IF YOU'RE COUNTRY...

EVERYBODY LOVES CHASIN' A BUCK.

A **DRIVE-THRU** IS THE EASIEST WAY TO PICK UP YOUR VEGGIE BURGER IF YOU FORGOT TO WEAR PANTS.

IF YOU'RE COUNTRY...

A *DRIVE-THRU* IS WHAT YOU DO WITH THE RIGHT TIRES AND THE RIGHT MUD HOLE.

IF YOU'RE COUNTRY...

AND YOU'RE TIRED OF WALKIN' IN THE WOODS, FIND AN OLD LOG. IT'S NOT MUCH, BUT AT LEAST IT'S SOMETHIN' TO PUT YOUR **KNEE ON**.

IF YOU'RE **CITY**...

AND YOUR COMPUTER IS TURNED OFF, YOU SHOULD **BOOT UP** IT!

IF YOU'RE COUNTRY...

AND A CITY BOY IS BEIN' A BUTT, YOU SHOULD PUT A **BOOT UP** IT.

"If You're City, If You're Country" CD

1. The Country Boy Song
(Earl Dibbles Jr., Tyler Smith, Matt Caldwell, Chris Gainz)
© 2013 Isla Blue Music, LLC (BMI) admin by Colton Music, LLC dba Colton Sounds, Red Tractor Publishing (BMI) admin by Me Gusta Music, Dixie Stars Music (ASCAP) admin by HoriPro Entertainment Group, Inc., Popaloo Music (BMI) admin by Me Gusta Music. All rights reserved. Used by permission.

2. Country Boy Love
(Earl Dibbles Jr.)
© 2013 Climbing Windmills Music (BMI) admin by Warner-Tamerlane Publishing Corp., Warner-Tamerlane Publishing Corp. (BMI). All rights reserved. Used by permission.

3. City Boy Stuck
(Earl Dibbles Jr., Austin Outlaw, Tyler Smith, Chris Gainz)
© 2015 Climbing Windmills Music (BMI) admin by Warner-Tamerlane Publishing Corp., Warner-Tamerlane Publishing Corp. (BMI), House of Sea Gayle Music (ASCAP) admin by ClearBox Rights, Spirit Two Nashville (ASCAP) obo Spirit Catalog Holdings S.à.r.l., Red Tractor Publishing (BMI) admin by Me Gusta Music, Popaloo Music (BMI) admin by Me Gusta Music. All rights reserved. Used by permission.

4. Merica
(Earl Dibbles Jr., Austin Outlaw, Chris Gainz, Dusty Saxton)
© 2016 Climbing Windmills Music (BMI) admin by Warner-Tamerlane Publishing Corp., Warner-Tamerlane Publishing Corp. (BMI), Fluid Tunes (ASCAP) admin by Spirit Two Nashville, Spirit Two Nashville (ASCAP), Popaloo Music (BMI) admin by Me Gusta Music, Dustin Saxton Music (BMI) admin by Me Gusta Music. All rights reserved. Used by permission.

5. Don't Tread on Me
(Earl Dibbles Jr., Austin Outlaw, Chris Gainz)
© 2017 Warner-Tamerlane Publishing Corp. (BMI), Climbing Windmills Music (BMI) admin by Warner-Tamerlane Publishing Corp., Spirit Two Nashville (ASCAP), Fluid Tunes (ASCAP) admin by Spirit Two Nashville, Popaloo Music (BMI) admin by Me Gusta Music. All rights reserved. Used by permission.

6. If You're Country, If You're City audiobook, read by Earl Dibbles Jr.
(Earl Dibbles Jr.)
© 2018 Granger Smith, BMG Books. All rights reserved. Used by permission.